**DATE DUE**

| | | | |
|---|---|---|---|
| MAR 08 02 | | | |
| MR 21 '05 | | | |
| | | | |
| | | | |
| | | | |
| | | | |
| | | | |
| | | | |
| | | | |
| | | | |

# Overcoming the Odds

# Monica Seles

### Suzanne J. Murdico

RSVP

**RAINTREE
STECK-VAUGHN**
P U B L I S H E R S
The Steck-Vaughn Company

*Austin, Texas*

Published by Raintree Steck-Vaughn Publishers,
an imprint of Steck-Vaughn Company

Developed for Steck-Vaughn Company by
Visual Education Corporation, Princeton, New Jersey
Editor: Marilyn Miller
Photo Research: Marty Levick
Electronic Preparation: Cynthia C. Feldner, *Manager;* Fiona Torphy
Production Supervisor: Ellen Foos
Electronic Production: Lisa Evans-Skopas, *Manager;*
Elise Dodeles, Deirdre Sheean, Isabelle Verret
Interior Design: Maxson Crandall

**Raintree Steck-Vaughn Publishers staff**
Editor: Kathy DeVico
Project Manager: Joyce Spicer

Photo Credits: **Cover:** © ALLSPORT; **4:** © ALLSPORT; **7:** © REUTERS/STR/Archive Photos;
**8:** © REUTERS/STR/Archive Photos; **11:** © Kevin Kolczynski/*Sports Illustrated;*
**13:** © Kevin Kolczynski/*Sports Illustrated;* **14:** © Kevin Kolczynski/*Sports Illustrated;*
**19:** © Mike Blake/REUTERS/Archive Photos; **21:** © Scott Halleran/ALLSPORT;
**24:** © ALLSPORT; **27:** © AP/Wide World Photos, Inc.; **29:** © AP/Wide World Photos, Inc.;
**31:** © AP/Wide World Photos, Inc.; **32:** © Simon Bruty/ALLSPORT;
**37:** © AP/Wide World Photos, Inc.; **38:** © AP/Wide World Photos, Inc.;
**39:** © Simon Bruty/ALLSPORT; **40:** © Matthew Stockman/ALLSPORT;
**41:** © Gary M. Prior/ALLSPORT; **42:** © Simon Bruty/ALLSPORT

Library of Congress Cataloging-in-Publication Data
Murdico, Suzanne J.
    Monica Seles / Suzanne J. Murdico.
        p.    cm. — (Overcoming the odds)
    Includes bibliographical references (p. 46) and index.
    Summary: A biography of the tennis star known for her two-handed grip who
beat the odds after being stabbed in the back at the 1993 Citizen Cup tournament
in Hamburg, Germany.
    ISBN 0-8172-4128-0 (hardcover)
    ISBN 0-8172-8001-4 (softcover)
    1. Seles, Monica, 1973– —Juvenile literature.    2. Tennis players—Yugoslavia—
Biography—Juvenile literature.    3. Women tennis players—Yugoslavia—
Biography—Juvenile literature.    [1. Seles, Monica, 1973–.    2. Tennis players.
3. Women—Biography.]    I. Title.    II. Series.
GV994.S45M87  1998
796.342´092—dc21
[B]                                                                         97–16807
                                                                              CIP
                                                                              AC

Printed and bound in the United States
1  2  3  4  5  6  7  8  9  0    WZ    01  00  99  98  97

# Table of Contents

# Chapter 1

## A Terrible Crime

Mon–i–ca! mon–i–ca! mon–i–ca!" More than 10,000 fans at the 1995 Canadian Open tennis tournament greeted Monica Seles by chanting her name and clapping. They were thrilled to see the 21-year-old tennis star. It had been 28 months since Monica competed in a professional tennis tournament. Many people had wondered if she would ever play tennis again.

The fans at the Canadian Open were not disappointed. Monica played tennis as if she had never been away. She defeated all five opponents without losing a set. In women's tennis a player wins a match by winning two out of three sets. The first player to win six games and lead by two games gains the set.

Monica had greatly missed playing tennis. After winning the Canadian Open, she said, "Deep inside I always knew I'd be back. I knew I would because I love the game so much."

When Monica left the sport in the spring of 1993, she was only 19 years old. She had been ranked the number one women's tennis player in the world

A smiling Monica grasps her trophy after beating Steffi Graf in the 1990 French Open in May. The victory was Monica's first Grand Slam win.

for two years. And she had already won eight Grand Slam events. These are the most important events in tennis—the Australian Open, the French Open, Wimbledon (in England), and the U.S. Open.

Monica was at the top of her game. But a terrible crime nearly cost her her life. It also forced Monica to leave the game she loved.

April 30, 1993, was a chilly day in Hamburg, Germany. Monica was playing in the quarterfinals at the Citizen Cup tournament. Eight players reach the quarterfinals, two players competing against each other in four matches. The four winners go on to the two semifinal matches, with the winners here competing against each other in the one finals match.

Now, about 7,000 spectators watched as Monica and Magdalena Maleeva of Bulgaria whacked the tennis ball back and forth across the court. It was the last quarterfinal match of the day. Monica had taken the first set 6–4 over Maleeva. In the second set, Monica was leading 4–3. In the middle of the match, the players took a one-minute break, called a changeover.

During the changeover Monica sat down on a chair to towel off and rest. Her chair was at the edge of the court, and she had her back to the stadium. Suddenly, without warning, Monica felt a sharp pain shoot through her back. She screamed and twisted around in her chair.

At that moment Monica saw a man standing behind her. He was holding a long knife in both hands.

Monica could see blood on the knife. Then Monica realized that the man was starting to lunge toward her! Fortunately a nearby security guard saw the man and quickly grabbed him. The guard pulled the man away from Monica.

As the security guard wrestled with her attacker, Monica jumped to her feet. She clutched at her back. As she struggled to understand what had happened, a spectator jumped onto the court to help her. The man caught Monica by the shoulders as she dropped to the ground in tears. Tournament officials ran to her aid. "Am I hurt? Am I bleeding?" Monica asked.

In the stands behind Monica, thousands of spectators knew the answer. They could see the bright-red blood spreading down and across the back of Monica's white shirt.

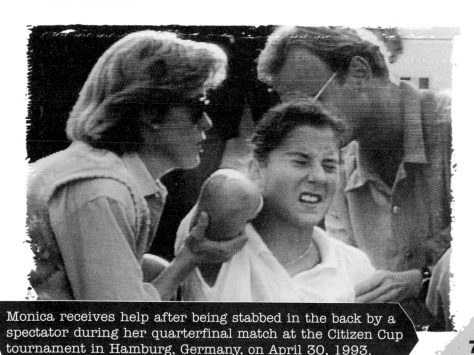

Monica receives help after being stabbed in the back by a spectator during her quarterfinal match at the Citizen Cup tournament in Hamburg, Germany, on April 30, 1993.

Zoltan Seles rushed to his sister's side. When she saw her brother, Monica calmed down a little. Paramedics soon arrived, and they put the injured player on a stretcher. They wheeled Monica out of the stadium and took her to the hospital. Because Monica clearly could not finish the match, it was ruled that she was out of the tournament.

At the hospital doctors examined Monica's back. She had a stab wound that was a half-inch deep. It was just below her right shoulder blade and a few inches from her spinal cord.

Dr. Richard Hawkins treated Monica. He explained that she was lucky to have been sitting down when the attack occurred. If she had been standing or had turned a different way, her injuries might have been much worse. Dr. Hawkins said that the knife could have entered a lung or the rib cage, which would have been "serious indeed."

At the time of the stabbing, Monica had no idea why anyone wanted to harm her. Later she discovered that her attacker, who had been arrested, was a German named Gunter Parche. He was an obsessed fan of German tennis star Steffi Graf.

Graf was Monica's main rival on the tennis court. She had been ranked the number one player in the world for several years. But Monica won many tournaments and eventually took over the number one position. That left Graf in the number two spot.

Gunter Parche was upset that Monica had taken the top ranking from Graf, his idol. He told the police that he wanted to injure Monica so that she could not play tennis. Then Steffi Graf could reclaim the number one ranking.

At the hospital the doctors told Monica that her physical injuries were not life-threatening. They said that the stab wound would probably heal in a few weeks. What they didn't know was that the knife attack would cause long-term psychological damage. In other words the stabbing had a negative effect on Monica's feelings and thoughts.

No one could have predicted it then, but the tennis world's number one player was going to be away from the game for a long time. It would be more than two years before Monica Seles would make her triumphant return at the Canadian Open.

# Chapter 2

## A Star Is Born

Monica Seles was born in Novi Sad, Yugoslavia, on December 2, 1973. Yugoslavia was a country in Eastern Europe. In 1991 it broke up into two countries—Serbia and Montenegro. Novi Sad is in Serbia. Monica's father, Karolj, was a cartoonist and documentary filmmaker. He won several awards for his work. Monica's mother, Esther, worked as a computer programmer.

Monica's older brother, Zoltan, liked to watch Swedish tennis legend Bjorn Borg on television. One day Zoltan decided that he wanted to play tennis like Borg. So he asked his father for a tennis racket.

Mr. Seles had been a top athlete in the triple jump, a track-and-field event. But he did not know how to play tennis. So he bought a racket for Zoltan and a paperback book on how to play the game. Armed with this instruction book and a knowledge of athletics, Mr. Seles began coaching Zoltan.

When Monica was only six years old, she decided that she wanted to play tennis, too. So Monica's father bought her a tennis racket. Monica recalled that

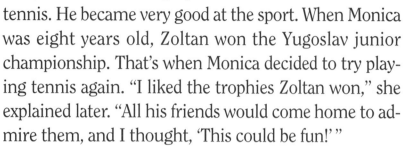

Monica's family—her parents and her brother, Zoltan—have nurtured her tennis career, standing beside her every step of the way on her climb to the top.

she played for only two weeks. Then she put the racket down because she became tired of playing.

Monica's brother, however, continued to play tennis. He became very good at the sport. When Monica was eight years old, Zoltan won the Yugoslav junior championship. That's when Monica decided to try playing tennis again. "I liked the trophies Zoltan won," she explained later. "All his friends would come home to admire them, and I thought, 'This could be fun!'"

Monica started practicing for an hour before school and a few hours after school. She hit tennis balls against the brick wall of the family's apartment building.

The town where the family lived had only a few tennis courts. So Monica, her father, and her brother hung a net between the rows of cars in the apartment parking lot. It was not easy to play tennis on this makeshift court, but they enjoyed themselves anyway.

Mr. Seles found a creative way to encourage his daughter to play tennis. Monica's favorite cartoon characters were Tom and Jerry. So Monica's father drew pictures of Jerry (a mouse) on the tennis balls, and he drew Tom (a cat) on her T-shirts. Monica pretended that she was Tom chasing after Jerry.

Mr. Seles also placed stuffed animals on the court so that Monica could aim at them. When Monica played well, she received dolls as prizes.

Mr. Seles taught Monica, who is left-handed, to grip the racket with two hands for both her backhand and forehand strokes. Many players use a two-fisted backhand, but a two-fisted forehand is very unusual. Monica continues to use it today. This technique enables her to hit the ball from both sides with great force.

Mr. Seles's coaching strategies clearly paid off. At age 9 Monica became the Yugoslav 12-and-under champion. A year later she won the European 12-and-under championship. In 1985, 11-year-old Monica was named Yugoslavian Sportswoman of the Year. She was the first person younger than 18 to receive that honor.

Another important event happened in 1985. Monica traveled to Miami, Florida, to compete in the Orange Bowl 12-and-under tournament. Monica won the tournament, and famed tennis coach Nick Bollettieri saw her win it.

Bollettieri knew a promising player when he saw one. He offered Monica a full scholarship to the Nick Bollettieri Tennis Academy in Bradenton, Florida.

It was a big decision, but Mr. and Mrs. Seles wanted their daughter to take advantage of this great opportunity. In 1986 Monica and Zoltan moved from Yugoslavia to Florida. They lived at the tennis academy.

Coach Nick Bollettieri works with Monica on her forehand.

Their parents decided to stay in Yugoslavia and to continue working in order to support the family.

Six months later, however, Mr. and Mrs. Seles quit their jobs and left Yugoslavia. They moved into a two-bedroom apartment near the tennis academy. At that time Monica's parents spoke very little English. Monica and Zoltan had learned some English in school.

Monica worked hard at the academy, practicing six hours a day. She played aggressively, hitting the ball so hard that the other girls at the academy didn't want to practice with her. So Monica was matched with boys instead. She even practiced with future champions Andre Agassi and Jim Courier, both of the United States.

Jim Courier remembers an early encounter with Monica. Coach Bollettieri had asked him to practice with her. But Monica seemed more interested in winning than in practicing. During their "practice" session, the 12-year-old whacked shot after shot past Courier.

Monica was not only a top-notch tennis student; she had an A average at Bradenton Academy.

"After 15 minutes I walked off," says Courier. "I told Nick, never again. He could get another guinea pig."

Although Monica spent many hours each day practicing tennis, she also attended school. She was an A student at Bradenton Academy. Like most young people, Monica had dreams of what she wanted to be when she grew up. First, she wanted to be a great tennis player. She also imagined being a lawyer, a journalist, a model, and an actress.

During these early years, Monica did not participate in any junior tournaments. Bollettieri wanted to show off the talent of his star pupil. But Monica's parents wanted to keep their daughter's unusual playing style hidden from her opponents. They were waiting until Monica was ready to play in professional tennis tournaments. That day would come soon.

# Chapter 3

## From Amateur to Professional

In March 1988 Monica was ready for her first professional tournament, the Virginia Slims competition in Boca Raton, Florida. Even though Monica was still an amateur, she was eligible to play in the tournament. All the top women players were invited to compete. In this event Monica played against Helen Kelesi of Canada. During the match tennis champions Chris Evert of the United States and Steffi Graf observed from the stands. They wanted to watch Monica—a young newcomer who was playing very well.

The winner of the Seles-Kelesi match would play Evert in the next round. With these great players watching, Monica was a bit nervous. She still upset the 35th-ranked Kelesi, winning two sets by the score of 7–6 and 6–3.

In the next round, Monica played against Evert. Evert is 19 years older than Monica. Although Monica lost the match, she was thrilled just to have competed against one of her childhood idols. At that time Monica was only 14 years old. She stood just 5 feet 4 inches tall and weighed a mere 100 pounds.

A week after the Virginia Slims tournament, Monica played in the Lipton International Players' Championships in Key Biscayne, Florida. She won the first match easily. In the second match, Monica competed against fourth-ranked Gabriela Sabatini of Argentina. Although Monica lost 7–6, 6–3, she played well. People were starting to notice this talented young player.

The requirements for women players to turn professional are complicated. But Monica fulfilled all of them, and in February 1989 she gave up her amateur status. One big reason for this decision was that as a professional, she would be able to earn prize money, something she could not do as an amateur.

Her first tournament as a professional was the Virginia Slims competition in Washington, D.C. Monica easily defeated her first two opponents and advanced to the quarterfinals. She was matched against Manuela Maleeva, who was ranked in the top ten. Monica was ranked 88th.

In the first set, Monica defeated Maleeva 6–2. The second set was not so easy. Monica sprained her ankle and was in a lot of pain. She still managed not only to continue playing but also to win the set 6–4 and, with it, the match. This meant that she would move on to the semifinals.

Now Monica had to make a difficult decision. Should she play in the semifinals with a sprained ankle? The match was important, and she really wanted to play. But Monica decided not to take the chance of hurting herself even more.

Monica's first major victory came in April 1989, just two months after she turned professional. At the Virginia Slims tournament in Houston, Texas, she breezed through the early rounds. In the final round, Monica was once again matched against Chris Evert.

Evert took the first set 6–3. Then Monica rallied to win the second set 6–1. The winner of the third set would win the match. With a score of 6–4, Monica defeated Evert and won the championship.

Monica's first Grand Slam event was the 1989 French Open. When Monica appeared at Roland Garros Stadium in Paris, she made a grand entrance. Just before the tournament, she had dyed her brown hair blond. Then, as she walked onto the court, she waved to the crowd and threw roses up into the stands.

Monica's growing number of fans loved the 15-year-old's friendliness and her unique style. Monica enjoyed wearing designer outfits and sometimes even disguised herself off court in a hat or a wig.

Many people thought that she brought a breath of fresh air to a sport that had become a bit predictable. One sportscaster called Monica "bigger than life." Not everyone was as enthusiastic, however. Chris Evert described Monica as "a drama queen."

No matter what people thought of Monica's personality, they were certainly impressed by her talent. Monica had no trouble winning the first few rounds of the French Open. After defeating Manuela Maleeva in the quarterfinals, she advanced to the semifinal round. There she would meet Steffi Graf.

Monica was thrilled. In her first Grand Slam event, she had made it all the way to the semifinals. Graf took the first set 6–3. Then Monica started to relax, and she won the second set 6–3.

The crowd was excited. Even most of the top ten players did not compete this well against the great Steffi Graf. No one expected Monica, a relatively unknown player, to take a set from this champion.

In the third set, the players were tied at three games each. Eventually, though, Graf triumphed in the match by winning the set 6–3. Although Monica lost, she was not disappointed. She knew that she had played well. She was confident that someday she would come back to win this tournament.

Throughout 1989 Monica competed in many other tournaments. Two were Grand Slam events—Wimbledon and the U.S. Open. Monica did not triumph in any other major tournaments that year. But she established herself as a major player.

Monica was becoming well known for two other aspects of her personality beside her tennis ability—giggling and grunting. Monica giggles a lot, and her laugh has been compared to Woody Woodpecker's. Her grunting occurs when she whacks a tennis ball across a court. Many tennis players grunt when they breathe out as they hit the ball. But Monica's grunt

Monica grunts as she returns a shot with the great power she is known for.

is especially loud because she hits the ball with such great force.

During 1989 Monica did something that she had dreamed about her whole life. She played against two of her childhood heroines—Martina Navratilova and Chris Evert. When Monica was six, she had watched Navratilova and Evert play. Now she was actually playing against them. It seemed very strange to her. But Monica was soon to move on to even greater accomplishments.

# Chapter 4

## On the Way to Number One

In December 1989 Monica turned 16. Since becoming a professional, she had risen in the rankings of female players from number 88 to number 6. Monica had performed so well in that first year of professional competition that people expected her to play even better in 1990.

But the new year did not start off well for Monica. In February she suffered a first-round loss at the Virginia Slims tournament in Chicago, Illinois. At the Virginia Slims competition in Washington, D.C., however, she advanced through the first three rounds. Then Martina Navratilova defeated her in the semifinals. Monica started to worry that maybe expectations for her had been too high. Maybe she couldn't live up to them.

In March 1990 Monica attended the Lipton International Players' Championships in Key Biscayne, Florida. That's when events started to turn around for the teenager. She defeated all six opponents to win the tournament. She went on to win two more championships in March and April.

Although Monica was on a winning streak, she had her share of problems. In the spring of 1990, she had a bitter breakup with her coach, Nick Bollettieri.

The Seles family began to feel that Bollettieri was not spending enough time coaching Monica. They thought that he was concentrating too much on his other up-and-coming player, Andre Agassi. Although Bollettieri disagreed, Monica's father took over as his daughter's coach.

Other changes were also challenging Monica. She grew 5 inches taller. At 5 feet 9 inches, she now looked at the world—and tennis—from a new vantage point. "The net seemed a different height, and the racket seemed lighter, like I was playing Ping-Pong," she explained. This growth spurt forced Monica to relearn her game.

To many observers Monica does not look like a typical athlete. She is not into physical fitness as much as some other tennis champions, including Steffi Graf. Monica, however, is able to hit the ball with enormous strength. At a speed of more than 100 miles per hour, Monica's serve is incredibly fast.

In May 1990 Monica entered her next major tournament, the Italian Open. She dominated her opponents in the first four rounds. In the finals she again faced one of her great rivals, Navratilova. Unlike their last encounter, though, Monica was in control of this match. She easily defeated Navratilova 6–1, 6–1. Afterward Navratilova told reporters, "It was like being run over by a truck."

Monica was now consistently beating the other top-ranked tennis players. She still had one major opponent left to defeat, however. That player was Steffi Graf, who was ranked number one in the world. Monica met that challenge at the German Open in May 1990.

Monica and Graf won their early rounds and faced each other in the finals. Although both young women played great tennis, Monica was victorious. She was as surprised as everyone else. Monica later wrote in her autobiography, "Nobody had expected me to beat Steffi—she was the unbeatable one."

Graf certainly hadn't expected to lose the match. She was very upset. According to Monica, Graf hit a wall so hard with her racket that it left a large hole.

Meanwhile, Monica was proving that her winning streak was not just a matter of good luck. One more important victory was still outstanding, though. Monica had yet to win a Grand Slam event.

The French Open is one of the four Grand Slam events in tennis. In June 1990 Monica traveled to Paris to compete in this tournament. After winning in the early rounds of play, she advanced to the semifinals.

For that match she competed against a rising young star—Jennifer Capriati. Capriati was only 14 years old. The press labeled this semifinal match "the battle of two children."

Capriati was a newcomer who had played in just a few major tournaments. Although Monica was only 16, she had the advantage of more tournament experience than Capriati. Monica won the match by the score of 6–2, 6–2.

In the finals Monica once again found herself facing Graf. Monica was determined to win. In the first set, she was leading 3–1. Then rain caused a delay of nearly an hour.

When the players returned to the court, Graf tied the score at 3–3. After the next few games, the score was tied again at 6–6. In this tournament a score of 6–6 meant that the players would have to play a tiebreaker. In a tiebreaker the first player to reach 7 points wins the set. Like all great tennis players, both Monica and Steffi are fierce competitors, fighting for every point in a match. But this time Monica fought a little harder than Steffi and won the tiebreaker.

Now Monica had the mental advantage of having taken the first set. In the second set, she defeated Graf by the score of 6–4. Monica had won her first Grand Slam event. This victory also put her in the history books. Monica became the youngest woman ever to

win the French Open. She also was the youngest player to win a Grand Slam event in more than 100 years.

After the French Open, Monica moved up to number three in the world rankings. In July 1990 she went to England to play at Wimbledon, another Grand Slam event. Although Monica made it into the quarterfinals, she was defeated there by Zina Garrison of the United States in three sets. This loss put an end to Monica's winning streak of six straight tournaments.

In September Monica played in her third Grand Slam event of the year—the U.S. Open. She easily won the first two rounds. The third round went to three sets, but Monica lost to Linda Ferrando of Italy.

Although she was disappointed with her own performance, Monica knew that she had to accept the loss and move past it. She went on to win two Virginia Slims tournaments at the end of 1990. "It was a funny kind of year," Monica recalled later. "I had some radical success and some radical disappointment."

By the end of the year, Monica had climbed to number two in the rankings. Graf maintained the number one position. Monica had won nine tournaments and more than $1.6 million in prize and bonus money for the year. *Tennis* magazine named her the most improved female professional of 1990.

Monica was in an excellent position heading into 1991. She sailed through the early rounds of the Australian Open in January, easily defeating her opponents. In the semifinals she faced Mary Joe Fernandez of the United States. As Monica recalled later, the temperature on the court was a broiling 134°F (57°C). Playing in such heat made exhaustion a real possibility for the players.

Although Monica won the first set, Fernandez rallied to take the second set. In the third set, the score was tied at 7–7, until Monica broke through to pull out the match 9–7.

In the finals of the Australian Open, Monica faced Jana Novotna of the Czech Republic. Novotna won the first set by the score of 7–5. But she could not keep her opponent down. Monica came roaring back to take the next two sets 6–3 and 6–1. Now Monica had won her second Grand Slam tournament.

Monica's many championship victories allowed her to seize the number one ranking from Graf in March 1991. Graf had held that position for a record 186 weeks, or more than 3½ years. At 17 years and 3 months old, Monica became the youngest tennis player ever to gain the number one ranking.

Now the stage was set for a new phase in the epic battle between Monica Seles and Steffi Graf. Their rivalry was compared with that of Martina Navratilova and Chris Evert in the 1980s. Could Monica hold on to the number one spot? Or would Graf reclaim it? Only time would tell.

# Chapter 5

## The Winning Streak Continues

In May 1991 Monica flew to Paris to compete in her second French Open. Because she was playing well and had won the event the previous year, expectations were high. Monica did not disappoint herself or her fans. In the semifinals she defeated Gabriela Sabatini 6–4, 6–1.

Monica had expected to face Graf in the finals. But Graf had been beaten by Arantxa Sanchez Vicario of Spain in their semifinal match. With the score of 6–3, 6–4, Monica went on to take the final match against Sanchez Vicario. That win clinched Monica's second consecutive French Open title.

If Monica could win the 1991 Wimbledon tournament, it would be her third Grand Slam victory in a row. If she then went on to victory in the U.S. Open, she would have won all four events in a single year. That would earn her a complete Grand Slam. In the history of the sport, only three women had achieved that honor. They were Maureen Connolly of the United States (1953), Margaret Smith Court of Australia (1970), and Steffi Graf (1988).

But it did not happen for Monica. She had to withdraw from Wimbledon unexpectedly. Monica had developed shinsplints and a stress fracture in her left leg. These injuries caused her great pain when she ran.

It is not unusual for athletes to become injured and pull out of competitions. However, Monica waited until the last minute to announce her withdrawal from Wimbledon. Then she disappeared from the public eye for nearly two weeks. That was unusual.

The press began to wonder what had happened to the world's number one player. Newspapers printed many differing stories about Monica. Most of them were not true. The truth was that she had entered a rehabilitation clinic to recover from her injuries.

While she was recovering from her injuries, Monica and her dog Astro met with reporters on July 18, 1991, at the Pathmark Tennis Classic in New Jersey.

Monica recovered from her injuries and was soon ready to play tennis again. In September she competed in the U.S. Open in Flushing, New York. One of the most exciting matches of the tournament was the semifinal round between Monica and Jennifer Capriati.

Only one month before the U.S. Open, Capriati had beaten Monica at another tournament. As an American playing at the U.S. Open, Capriati was the favorite. The crowd was cheering for her. These factors could have put Monica at a disadvantage. But she did not let herself become distracted.

Both teenagers fought like tigers for every point. *Tennis* magazine called the match "a three-set slugfest." Monica eventually beat Capriati by winning a third-set tiebreaker. Monica then advanced to the finals.

Navratilova had defeated Graf to advance to the final round. There she faced Monica, and Monica prevailed. She defeated Navratilova in two sets by the score of 7–6 and 6–1. This was Monica's first victory at the U.S. Open. She had now won three of the four Grand Slam titles in 1991.

Monica went on to win several other tournaments in the fall. In the end 1991 turned out to be an exceptional year for the young player. She participated in 16 events and made it to the finals in every event. She gained ten titles, including the three Grand Slams.

Monica's amazing winning streak continued into 1992. In January she played in the Australian Open.

In the final round, she defeated Mary Joe Fernandez in two sets. This was Monica's second straight victory at the Australian Open.

Monica played in several more championships before heading to the French Open in June. If she won that tournament, she would become the first woman in more than 50 years to win three straight French Open titles.

Winning the French Open turned out to be a real struggle. As early as the fourth round, Monica started having trouble. Akiko Kijimuta of Japan, ranked 150th, won the second set, forcing Monica to play a third set before she won the match.

The semifinal round also went to three sets. Monica took the first set 6–3, but her opponent, Gabriela Sabatini, fought back to win the second set 6–4. In the third set, Monica was trailing 4–2. It took all her courage and endurance to overcome her fatigue and pull the set out 6–4, to win the match.

The final round of the French Open was the showdown that the world wanted to see: Seles versus Graf. The two players were so evenly matched that the round lasted nearly three hours. Monica won the first set 6–2. But Graf rallied to take the second set 6–3.

By the third set, both players were even more determined to win. The score was tied at 6–6 and again at 8–8. Ultimately Monica broke the tie and won the final set 10–8. Monica felt that was the hardest she ever had to work for a Grand Slam title.

After earning her third French Open title, Monica hoped to win her first Wimbledon championship. Wimbledon, the most important tennis event in England, was the only Grand Slam title that she had not won.

As Monica began to eliminate her opponents in the early rounds, the news media started to focus on her grunting. A great deal of attention was paid to the loudness of her grunts at Wimbledon.

Perhaps it was because some of Monica's opponents began to complain about the noise. In the semifinals Navratilova said that the grunting was so loud that she could not hear the ball being hit. An official warned Monica to tone it down. Monica defeated Navratilova anyway, but the complaints were distracting her.

In Monica's autobiography she explained what happened next. "When I stepped onto center court to play Steffi Graf in the Wimbledon finals, I only thought about one thing: Don't grunt. It was one of the biggest mistakes I've ever made." Concentrating on not grunting caused Monica to lose focus on the game. Graf took the Wimbledon championship in straight sets 6–2, 6–1. Monica never made the same mistake again.

In September Monica played in her third U.S. Open tournament. In seven rounds she never lost a set. She defeated Sanchez Vicario 6–3, 6–3 in the finals. Monica had won her second consecutive U.S. Open championship and her seventh Grand Slam title.

At the start of 1993, Monica was on top of the world. Only 19 years old, she was winning match after match. She had held the number one ranking for nearly two years.

In January Monica traveled to Melbourne to defend her title for the second time at the Australian Open. She defeated her opponents in the early rounds and then won the semifinals against Sabatini. For the final match, Monica once again faced her fiercest rival, Steffi Graf.

On August 31, 1992, Monica was honored as the Women's Tennis Association's Player of the Year during ceremonies in New York City.

Coming into the finals, Graf looked strong. She had yet to give up any sets. In her first set with Monica, she continued to play well. Graf took the set 6–4. But Monica was not willing to let Graf reclaim her title. Reaching deep inside herself, Monica won the next two sets 6–3, 6–2. For the third time in a row, Monica was victorious at the Australian Open.

After losing the championship, Graf analyzed Monica's tennis strategy: "Once she gets in the groove, she just plays every point as hard as she can. . . . That is definitely her strength."

After playing two more tournaments in February, Monica found out that she had a bad viral infection. The doctor recommended total relaxation. Monica withdrew from the next few tournaments.

By April Monica had recovered from her illness and was ready to return to the tour. Only about one month remained before the French Open. To prepare for it, she needed to play in another tournament. So she entered the Citizen Cup in Hamburg, Germany. Of course, Monica had no way of knowing that her life was about to be turned upside down by a man she had never met.

Monica displays her Australian Open championship trophy before photographers in January 1993. She has just defeated Steffi Graf in three sets.

# Chapter 6

## Away from the Court

After Gunter Parche stabbed Monica Seles on April 30, 1993, the media spread the news around the world. People everywhere wanted to know why this man had committed such an awful crime. How did it happen in the middle of a tennis tournament? How could it have occurred in front of thousands of people? Could the attack have been prevented?

Monica also battled with her own personal concerns. Would she recover from her injuries? Would she still be able to play tennis? Would she ever again feel safe on a tennis court?

After the attack Monica stayed overnight at the hospital. Police officers patrolled the halls to ensure her safety. The next day Monica had a visitor—Steffi Graf. The two champions, who were not friends off the court, had an emotional meeting. Afterward Graf said that her rival was "very, very depressed."

The doctors were ready to release Monica after one night at the hospital. But she decided to stay a second night. The next day she flew to Vail, Colorado. There she checked into the Steadman-Hawkins clinic to begin a physical therapy program.

Many experts predicted that Monica's physical recovery would take a month or two. But Monica stayed at the Steadman-Hawkins clinic for six months. During that time she did exercises to regain full motion in her left shoulder.

She wasn't ready to play tennis for quite a while, though. Monica did not hit any balls until September. Then Dr. Steadman permitted her to hit two balls into a net set up in his office.

In the fall of 1993, Monica began working out with Bob Kersee and his wife, Jackie Joyner-Kersee. Bob is a famous track coach, and Jackie is an Olympic gold medalist in track and field. Monica worked on improving her upper-body strength. She also concentrated on "neglected aspects of my game, like volleying."

In October Monica received shocking news. The man who had stabbed her was free. In Germany, Gunter Parche had been tried for the crime of bodily injury rather than for the more serious crime of attempted murder. After he was found guilty, the judge had given him a suspended sentence. That meant that Parche did not have to go to jail.

How could the man who had nearly taken Monica's life be allowed to go free? Many people felt that Monica's refusal to testify against Parche hurt her case. But she had decided not to take the stand because that meant sitting in the courtroom with her back to him. In an American courtroom, Monica would have faced the defendant if she had testified.

By the end of 1993, Monica had physically recovered from the stab wound. She was also getting back in top tennis form. She even started talking about returning to the professional tennis tour.

During the Christmas holidays, Monica took a break from rehabilitation. For the first time since the stabbing, she had time to think. "I had to deal with emotions I didn't even know existed in my mind," she said.

That is when Monica started to have nightmares about the attack. She couldn't sleep and was afraid to leave the house. When fans told her that they missed her, she would start to cry. Monica's physical wounds had healed, but her emotional wounds ran much deeper. She sank into a deep depression.

In February 1994 Monica's father sat his daughter down and talked to her. He insisted that she go to a therapist. She needed to work through the fears and emotional problems that resulted from the attack.

Eventually Monica agreed and started to see a sports psychologist. Dr. Jerry Russell May treated her for post-traumatic stress disorder, which is characterized by nightmares, difficulty in sleeping, and sudden changes of mood. This condition is common in victims of violent attacks.

In March 1994 Monica made an important decision. The Yugoslavia-born tennis pro became a U.S. citizen. Monica and her mother took the citizenship test on the same day. Both passed. After they were sworn in as citizens that same year, Monica said, "I am proud to be a United States citizen and look forward to continuing our lives here."

Toward the end of 1994, after months of therapy with Dr. May, Monica finally started to put her life back together. She even began having fun again. She took French lessons and learned how to play the guitar.

Friends encouraged Monica to go jet-skiing and waterskiing. She enjoyed reading, shopping, and playing pool. Monica was beginning to come out of her depression.

During this time away from tennis, Monica attended several charity events. One of these was the 1994 Arete Awards, which honor courageous athletes. Monica presented an award to Sonya Bell, a 13-year-old blind gymnast. Bell's bravery was inspirational to Monica. At the 1995 Special Olympics World Games held in New Haven, Connecticut, in July, Monica gave tennis lessons to the athletes.

It is hard for some people to understand why Monica's recovery took more than two years. Monica explained that she felt as if she had lost control of her life. She also lived in fear. "The one place I felt safe was a tennis court—and that was taken away from me."

Monica shows a Special Olympics tennis player how to hit a forehand shot at the 1995 Special Olympics World Games in New Haven, Connecticut.

Many people had tried to persuade Monica to return to tennis earlier in her recovery. But Monica was waiting until she felt ready. "When I play tennis again, I have to play it for the right reason," she said. That reason was not the fame, the money, or even the fans. "I only want to play because I love the game, which is the reason I began to play in the first place."

In July 1995 Monica finally decided that she was ready to return to the sport she loved.

# Chapter 7

## A Triumphant Return

**M**onica chose to start her comeback slowly by entering an exhibition match. This type of match is played for fun (and money). But it does not count toward a player's competitive record.

The exhibition match was scheduled for July 29 in Atlantic City, New Jersey. Monica's opponent was tennis legend Martina Navratilova. Navratilova had retired from professional tennis the year before.

Monica was very nervous as she walked onto the court before their match. "My heart was pounding so hard that its beat filled my ears," she remembered.

An emotional Monica walks onto the court before the exhibition match in Atlantic City against Martina Navratilova on July 29, 1995, that marks Monica's return to tennis.

Monica waves to the crowd before beginning the exhibition match against Martina.

Monica was greeted by the thunderous applause of the crowd. Then she knew that she was back where she belonged. " 'I'm home,' I thought as I walked out, 'I'm home.' "

In her nervousness Monica started the match by double-faulting, which means that the server misses her serve twice in a row and loses a point. After that, however, Monica's natural skills and abilities took over. She went on to defeat Navratilova by the score of 6–3, 6–2.

Now Monica was ready to face an even greater challenge—returning to the competitive tennis tour. The World Tennis Association decided to restore the number one ranking that Monica had held before the attack. She and Graf would share the number one ranking.

Monica was happy with this decision, but not everyone else was. Some of the other players felt that Monica had been away from tennis for too long to still be ranked number one.

The first tournament of Monica's return was the Canadian Open. "For me it's not important that Monica wins this tournament," her father said. "It's that Monica comes back and Monica smiles."

Monica surprised everyone, including herself, by making it into the finals. There she faced Amanda Coetzer of South Africa. In less than one hour, Monica crushed Coetzer 6–0, 6–1.

After her win at the Canadian Open, *Tennis* magazine wrote: "Monica Seles is back. And how." Now Monica faced her next major challenge—to play in a Grand Slam tournament. That happened a few weeks later at the U.S. Open.

Fans at the 1995 Canadian Open in August have their say about Monica's ranking.

When she arrived at the U.S. Open in New York, Monica was very worried. Although her first match wasn't until the evening, she started practicing at 7:00 A.M. She need not have been so concerned. Monica defeated her first opponent, Ruxandra Dragomir of Romania, 6–3, 6–1.

Monica continued to play well and advanced in the rounds. She made it to the semifinals and won that match against a top player, Conchita Martinez of Spain. The score was 6–2, 6–2.

Then came the match for which tennis fans had been waiting. Monica would face Steffi Graf in the finals of the U.S. Open. The fans were hoping for an exciting match, and these two players did not let them down.

Monica played tennis as well as she ever had— maybe even better. One sports reporter wrote, "The first set was the finest display of women's tennis I've ever seen." It went to a tiebreaker, and then Graf won the set, 7–6.

The press surrounds Monica during the U.S. Open in 1995.

Then Monica stormed back, trouncing Graf 6–0 in the second set. But Graf took the final set 6–3 to win the match. Although Monica lost the U.S. Open, she proved to herself and the world that she was back.

Even more important, Monica was having fun again. While in New York for the tournament, she saw two Broadway shows and a New York Giants football game. She even made a presentation at the MTV Music Awards.

At the U.S. Open, Monica had certainly shown that she had not lost her tennis ability. But she still felt that she had something to prove. In January 1996 she entered the Australian Open. Before the stabbing she had won this tournament three times in a row. If she triumphed again, she could almost forget that she had ever been away from tennis.

Monica eliminated her competition in the early rounds. In the semifinals she took on Chanda Rubin of the United States. It was a close match, but Monica won in three sets.

Advancing to the finals, Monica faced Anke Huber of Germany. By the score of 6–4, 6–1, Monica gained the match and her fourth Australian Open title. With this ninth Grand Slam victory, Monica's comeback was truly complete.

This win would remain the high point of 1996 for Monica. She suffered through several injuries and tournament losses during the rest of the year. In July she traveled to Atlanta, Georgia, to compete in her first Olympic Games. Because Monica had become an American citizen, she represented the United States. She went home without a medal, however, losing to Novotna, who was on the Czech Republic's team.

At the end of 1996, it remained to be seen if Monica would stay at the top of women's tennis. Would she be able to regain the dominance she had before the attack? To Monica the answer probably doesn't matter. For her, winning at tennis is not nearly as important as simply playing the game that nearly had been taken away from her. That she has returned to the game she loves, overcoming the memory of her stabbing, is triumph enough.

# Monica Seles's Career Highlights

**1983**   Won Yugoslav 12-and-under championship at age 9.

**1984**   Won European 12-and-under championship at age 10.

**1985**   At age 11, became the first person under age 18 to be named Yugoslavian Sportswoman of the Year.

**1986**   Moved from Yugoslavia to the United States.

**1988**   Played in first professional tournament at the Virginia Slims tournament in Florida.

**1989**   Turned professional in February.
Won professional tournament for the first time by defeating Chris Evert at the Virginia Slims tournament in Houston, Texas.

**1990**   Became the youngest woman to win the French Open and the youngest player in more than 100 years to win a Grand Slam event.
Named *Tennis* magazine's female Most Improved Pro.

**1991**   Became the youngest player to win the Australian Open.
Became the youngest tennis player to be ranked number one in the world.
Became the second-youngest player to win the U.S. Open (behind Tracy Austin of the United States).
Won three out of four Grand Slam events in the same year.
Named 1991 Associated Press Female Athlete of the Year.

**1992**   Became the first woman in more than 50 years to win three consecutive French Open titles.

**1993**   Stabbed during Citizen Cup tournament in Hamburg, Germany.

**1994**   Became a U.S. citizen.

**1995**   After a 28-month absence, returned to professional tennis and won the Canadian Open.

**1996**   Won fourth Australian Open title.
Competed in her first Olympic Games.

# Monica Seles's Grand Slam Record

| Year | Australian Open | French Open | Wimbledon | U.S. Open |
|------|-----------------|-------------|-----------|-----------|
| 1989 |                 | Semifinalist |          |           |
| 1990 |                 | Winner      | Quarterfinalist |     |
| 1991 | Winner          | Winner      | Withdrew  | Winner    |
| 1992 | Winner          | Winner      | Finalist  | Winner    |
| 1993 | Winner          | Injured     | Injured   | Injured   |
| 1994 | Injured         | Injured     | Injured   | Injured   |
| 1995 | Injured         | Injured     | Injured   | Finalist  |
| 1996 | Winner          | Quarterfinalist |       |           |

# Monica Seles's Career Earnings

| Year | Number of Tournaments | Earnings |
|------|-----------------------|----------|
| 1988 | 3 | $ 14,700 |
| 1989 | 12 | $ 239,361 |
| 1990 | 26 | $ 1,637,222 |
| 1991 | 21 | $ 2,457,758 |
| 1992 | 16 | $ 2,622,352 |
| 1993 | 6 | $ 437,588 |
| 1994 | 0 | $ 0 |
| 1995 | 2 | $ 397,010 |
| 1996* | 10 | $ 715,804 |
| Totals* | 96 | $8,521,795 |

*As of August 12, 1996.
SOURCE: COREL WTA TOUR Media Information System.

# Further Reading

Collins, Bud, and Zander Hollander, eds. *Bud Collins' Modern Encyclopedia of Tennis.* Detroit: Gale Research, 1994.

Harrington, Denis J. *Top 10 Women Tennis Players.* Springfield, NJ: Enslow Publishers, 1995.

Seles, Monica, and Nancy Ann Richardson. *Monica: From Fear to Victory.* New York: HarperCollins, 1996.

Singleton, Skip. *The Junior Tennis Handbook: A Complete Guide to Tennis for Juniors, Parents, and Coaches.* White Hall, VA: Shoe Tree Press, 1991.

Tym, Wanda. *The Illustrated Rules of Tennis.* Nashville, TN: Ideals Children's Books, 1995.

# Index

# Index cont.